# JOURNALING JOURNEYS

———— JOURNAL THROUGH THE JOURNEY ————
OF ENDING YOUR RELATIONSHIP WELL

Guided Journeys of Self-Exploration
to Gain Clarity and Purpose and
Transform Your Life

LINDA COOPER

Printed in the United States of America
ISBN-13: 978-1-7782837-1-0 (Paperback)

*This book is dedicated to the possibility of grace found within endings.*

*"We write to taste life twice, in the moment and in retrospect."*
*Anais Nin*

# CONTENTS

# JOURNALING JOURNEYS

Welcome to the Journaling Journey of working through ending your relationship well.

This is one of many journaling journeys created as guided journeys of self-exploration to gain clarity and insight through the writing process and do the necessary inner work that will transform your life.

This is an ongoing series of transformative guided journeys, which are listed at the end of this book. New journeys will be listed on www.inwardboundcoaching.com as well as www.amazon.com. and can be listened to on www.audible.com.

Each of us has a story that is created from the journey we take. What paths we choose, what choices we make along our journey, create our life.

It is my desire, in creating the *Journaling Journeys* series, to share with you my journey through many life transitions with the hope that you will see yourself in my journey and feel encouraged, supported, and know that you are not alone as we walk out this journey together.

This is not a book about how to journal and it is not a regular journal where you are on your own to sort through a list of questions. This is a shared experience of navigating the inner and outer experiences of change where I draw upon my own journey and combine it with my counseling and life coaching skills to assist you in your journey.

There is a feeling of hope and encouragement in knowing that another person has walked the same path as you and has successfully come out the other side. I know what you are going through, as I have experienced my version of the path you are walking.

I hope that this journey will give you the strength, courage, wisdom, and insight that will move you closer to yourself and your heart's desire.

*Linda*

# ABOUT THE AUTHOR

Linda Cooper

A little about my professional journey...

I am an author, life coach, and the founder of www.inward-boundcoaching.com where I provide tools, guidance, and self-empowerment skills to help women navigate the inner and outer landscape of change to create a richer, more fulfilling life.

Credentials

- Counselor for assaulted women and children
- Columnist for A Beautiful Life Magazine
- Transition Writing Specialist
- Certified Journal Facilitator
- Content and Course Creation at Karuna International, Inc.

- Resident Journal Facilitator at Karuna International, Inc.
- Faculty Member at the Therapeutic Writing Institute
- Certified Yoga Teacher
- Author of the upcoming book: The Somatic Success Factor

A little about my personal journey...

At age 53, I threw my life up in the air. After raising three children into adulthood, ending a 20-year marriage, and quitting an unfulfilling career, I sold my home and most of my belongings and began the task of re-creating my life. I wanted to create a life that would be more in alignment with who I was and who I was becoming.

When I let go of everything, there was a big void, a big wide open space that was waiting to be filled. I was on a journey of inner and outer exploration and so began to fill my life with travel. From the tundra of Iqaluit, Baffin Island, to the sights and flavors of Italy, to an Ashram in India, to a lion sanctuary in South Africa, I came alive, purging all my baggage and opening up to the adventure of living.

What travel did for me was to expand the parameters of what I knew. I needed to experience the vastness of the world, and as my inner and outer world became larger, so did my capacity to believe that there was more for me than I could envision with my limited perspective.

I had become credentialed throughout the years as a counselor and coach, had a love for writing, and was immersed in the process of walking and journaling through my journey of self-discovery and personal growth through my own lived experience.

My journey continues, as all of ours does, until the day we leave this earth. My path now is a more authentic path to who I am where I use my coaching, writing, and podcast experiences to share my expertise and experience with people looking to make changes in their own lives.

# WHY JOURNAL?

## My Journey

*"When I journal, I am not alone."*

Journaling has been a lifesaver in my life. Starting at the age of 13, my journal was the one safe place where I could go to be seen and heard. It was a place where I could give voice to my lived experience, where there were no repercussions, no judging and criticizing of who I was. It was a place where I could quietly "tell someone" how I was feeling on the inside; a place of refuge; where it was ok to be me; and where I could place all of the hurt and sadness that I could not hold inside of my body.

I did not journal because I wanted to; I journaled because I had to. It was my form of communication and where I tried to make sense of my world.

At 50+ my journal has been my constant companion through what has been a tumultuous journey through my teen years, two marriages, three children, letting go of my career, my home, and all of my belongings, and unraveling myself from my known reality in search of deeper meaning to my life.

I now share my journey to help women connect to their truth, explore themselves through journaling, and make the necessary changes to live the life they desire.

 **Your Journey:**

What has your journey been with journaling so far in your life?

# HOW TO USE THIS BOOK

This book has been created as a short introduction to the world of journaling as well as a tool to learn about reflective thinking and writing. It is also a guide to writing through your life transitions' internal and external experiences that you can use as a reference guide for future transitions.

Each chapter contains four sections based on a specific facet of the journaling journey we are looking at.

1. **My Journey**
2. **My Reflections**
3. **Your Journey**
4. **Your Reflections**

Each book in the series has a major theme and is then divided into various facets of the journey, where I share My Journey and My Reflections, and then invite you to follow the writing prompts in a separate notebook to record Your Journey and then work through Your Reflections.

Journaling Journeys can be used as a self-directed process, in conjunction with coaching, or with a professional therapist. It is not meant to replace therapy if you feel that is what you need.

## My Journey Section

Each *Journaling Journey* covers a different life transition that I have personally gone through. In this way, I am right here alongside you, sharing my learning, thoughts, and experiences.

*"My Journey"* is the sharing of my experience, which may not be exactly like your experience, but there may be commonalities that bring us together, and although I share my journey and insights, I do not have your answers. What I do, is pose questions as prompts in "Your *Journey*" so that you may begin to work through them to discover your truth and your answers.

## My Reflection Section

*"My reflection"* is a brief account of my reflective writing process where I share lessons learned and insights that arose from my journey.

Reflective writing is completed after you have initially written down your thoughts, feelings, and experiences. You revisit what you have written to now analyze the experience, recording how it has impacted you, the meaning it holds for you, as well as the learning you have gained that you can apply in the future.

## Your Journey Section

*"Your Journey"* is for you to get to know yourself, understand yourself, and gain clarity. Set some time aside and find a quiet space where you can read and ponder, and then, when ready, write out your responses to the prompts.

It is best to have your own notebook to use along with each Journaling Journey, where you will have the space needed to write out your answers, or if you prefer, to use your keyboard to type your answers into a private folder.

As you write, you may come up with more questions to ask yourself, which will allow you to explore even deeper. Go with the flow, and allow yourself to feel into your questions and your answers. Sit with them for a while and ponder. Carry them with you during your day to see if you can gain some more insights and clarity.

These *Journaling Journeys* are not meant to be completed in one sitting. Take your time, and keep adding to your responses as needed. This is a companion that will receive and hold your thoughts, feelings, and experiences, as well as your perceptions that may change as time passes.

You are on a journey of discovery, so be kind and gentle with yourself in this process. This is all about connecting to that deepest part of yourself, connecting to your truth, to your strength and courage that will help you navigate through the landscape of change to your success.

## Your Reflection Section

Journals are living documents of recorded thoughts, feelings, contemplations, and experiences and how they are perceived at the time of writing.

Perceptions can change, emotions can change, and circumstances can change, which is why it can be beneficial to re-read what you have written and write a reflection.

Through reflective writing, you are both the observer of your experience as well as the recorder of it. Allowing some time to pass from the initial writing and re-reading can give you more insights, time to add in more detail, and work through feelings and emotions to find those aha moments.

Learning from your experiences comes from your willingness and ability to truly see yourself, to be honest with yourself, and to see the bigger picture as well as the details. As you re-read what you have written, you will begin to see patterns of thought and behavior that have helped or hindered you.

Reflective writing invites deeper contemplation and introspection to learn more about yourself and to see where you may need to make some changes.

At the end of each facet of the journey, after you have completed writing out your responses to the prompts in the "*Your Journey*" section, there will be reflection prompts that you can use to guide you in exploring a bit deeper.

# WHERE ARE YOU IN YOUR JOURNEY TODAY?

Each day, each moment brings with it a circumstance, and circumstances can change in an instant. One moment, you are sitting enjoying a cup of tea, and the next moment, the phone rings, bringing you some bad news, and your emotions have switched gears.

We are affected by many variables around us, which will determine how we respond to circumstances we are faced with.

You may not have had a good sleep the night before. You may have had a conflict with a spouse or child that morning. You may have eaten something for dinner the night before that is sitting heavy in your system and you are feeling lethargic. You may have too many things on your to-do list and feel overwhelmed. There are a plethora of circumstances that will impact how you respond. This is no different when you are journaling.

The *Journaling Journeys* series is not meant to be completed all at once, or even just once, which is why it is best to have a separate notebook to work through the prompts.

Your responses may change depending on your mood, the time of day, the kind of day, and the impact that external and internal circumstances have on you.

These Journeys can be revisited as many times as needed. It is also helpful to read back what you have written at a later time and notice any differences in perspective, and perhaps continue your writing journey.

This is a journey of self-discovery you are on that will last a lifetime. There is no need to hurry through the prompts, you can set your own pace. Perhaps carry your journal with you so that if something comes to mind, you have your journal companion right there with you to record your thoughts and feelings.

Each time you open your journal, be mindful of all of the factors that will contribute to your responses, and perhaps you can begin your journaling by answering the question, *"Where am I, and what is affecting my journey today?"*

# JOURNAL THROUGH THE JOURNEY OF ENDING YOUR RELATIONSHIP WELL

## My Journey:

As I closed the front door and stepped out onto the porch into the evening, suitcase in hand, I paused and walked over to the big picture window and, with tear-filled eyes, looked in at the beautiful home I had created; the glass pane of the window separating me from what I most desired inside. This would be my first of five attempts to leave my relationship, or rather my five attempts to stay.

I stood in both awe and horror at my ability to create such beauty and my inability to sustain it. I paused for a moment to contemplate the magnitude of my decision. I did not want to leave, I had to.

I had stayed in this relationship to the detriment of my own health and well-being. I stayed for the children, I stayed for my spouse, I stayed for financial security, and I stayed because I truly loved my husband. I stayed because I didn't want to start all over again and I stayed because I was afraid to be alone.

But even with all of those reasons to stay, there came a point, much to my dismay, when the reasons to leave outweighed the reasons to stay. The reasons became necessities.

There were engrained patterns and coping mechanisms, along with perceptions and behaviors, that each of us brought to this relationship that would contribute to its demise.

We had both emerged from emotionally dysfunctional families of origin with wounds that would block us from having what we both so desired, healthy intimate relationships. As you will see as I bring you along, both of our buttons were being pushed continually in this relationship. From a therapeutic perspective, this could have been an opportunity to work through our pasts together, but we both carried such a magnitude of issues that the weight of it all was beyond our combined ability to repair it.

I will pause this journey here to give you a brief overview of our childhood experiences, as it gives context to the rest of the journey.

### My Childhood Story

If you opened the door and had a peek into my childhood home, you would not see anything out of the ordinary. You would see my mother, father, myself, and my sister going about daily life, but what you wouldn't see or feel was the tension of the unspoken sadness, hurt, and disappointment that I didn't have a language for back then. There were four people living under one roof, emotionally disconnected and spinning in their own suffering. You also wouldn't see the elephant in the living room. My father was a functioning alcoholic whose constant negativity, judgment, criticism, and lack of encouragement felt like death by a thousand cuts to my heart and my sense of worth and belonging.

Upon entering my teenage years, at the age of 14, I was sexually abused for a year and a half by my girlfriend's father, and at age 17, I was stalked, threatened with death, and sexually assaulted by a boyfriend I had broken up with. There had been no safe place in my life to tell anyone any of this, and so I remained *silent*, a pattern that would follow me into adulthood and most of my relationships.

Growing up without a feeling of connection, or having a soft place to fall, being in a house surrounded by people, and feeling all alone would also be a pattern that would haunt me continuously throughout my life.

## My Husband's Childhood Story

My husband was the third of seven children. He was conceived as a result of an extramarital affair with his mother's brother-in-law and was born with fetal alcohol syndrome. Twelve months later, a fourth child was conceived within the marriage, and then three more children were conceived by three different fathers. My husband was not born into a nurturing home. He was born into the storyline of a woman who was trying to find love and solace in men, in alcohol, prescription drugs, and in having babies. He was ostracized, ridiculed, bullied, and emotionally and physically abused by the man he thought was his father.

My husband is a gentle, sensitive soul who was not privy to the circumstances of his birth and so interpreted the way he was treated growing up as not being worthy of love. He grew up on the outside, not belonging, or having the role model of a healthy male or female relationship. Years later, he was to find out that the person he regarded as his father was not, but was not given any more information on his true identity at that time. His childhood years were spent watching men come and go, befriending him and then leaving. His mother would disappear regularly, and he would find himself searching for her, only to find her turn up in the arms of yet another man.

There were no adults to trust in his world. At age seven, his mother took him to the hospital where he was told he was going to have his eyes checked. Upon awaking, he was traumatized by temporary blindness for three days, having unknowingly received surgery to correct his inward-turning eyes due to fetal alcohol syndrome.

This was the little boy, now a grown man, who, at age 33, sat by his mother's side in the hospital as she lay dying of lung cancer, reading Ralph Waldo Emmerson to her, holding her hand, and telling her how much he loved her. This is the heart of the man that I fell in love with.

Traumatic life experiences in a child's early developmental stages leave life-long wounds. These experiences change who we are. These are the wounds that need our healing in order to create the life experience we desire.

When you come from a trauma history, your perceptions and the meaning you give to these circumstances can be skewed. The lens through which you look isn't necessarily the truth, it is your perception of the truth based on your lived experience and your interpretation of that experience.

In our relationship, I was not just dealing with my husband, nor was he just dealing with me. We were dealing with the outcome of our history, DNA, interpretations, and the meanings we assigned, all mushed together into each of our psyches.

As I share our journey, I want to state at the outset that my husband is a kind, generous, thoughtful, and gentle soul, and he was wounded, as was I. The sharing of our story is not to point fingers, to blame, shame, or position myself as the victim in this story, but rather to shine a light on how our life histories impacted our ability to have a healthy, intimate relationship. In both our cases, we were bringing much more into the marriage than we initially realized.

You do not marry a person, you marry a history of life experience encased in skin. You marry a lifetime of coping mechanisms formed into a personality. You marry into a family and an ancestral history that can greatly impact your success or failure as a couple.

**My Reflection:** *I emerged from my childhood with my fundamental coping mechanism being that silence equals safety. My husband emerged from his childhood having never experienced truth and transparency to find his security.*

## Your Journey:

1. How have your childhood experiences impacted your ability to have a healthy relationship?

2. Identify any coping mechanisms from childhood that are hindering your relationship.

3. How do you feel about your relationship?

4. Describe the issues in your relationship from your perspective.

5. What blocks you from having the relationship you desire?

6. How have your partner's childhood experiences affected your relationship? Do you know their whole story?

7. Describe the issues in your relationship from your partner's perspective.

8. What coping mechanisms used in your partner's childhood are not serving the relationship?

9. Where do you want to go from here?

## Your Reflection:

Having allowed some time to pass since working with the prompts and re-reading your responses, ask yourself:

What stands out for me is .....................................................

The recurring patterns I can see are ...........................................

My learning is ...............................................................

My next step will be .........................................................

## My Journey Continues:

**What we were each bringing into our relationship:**

Although we had different childhood experiences, there was an overlap in our coping mechanisms that grew out of these experiences.

My coping mechanisms from my childhood were:

- To not trust
- Emotional and physical withdrawal
- To be hypersensitive to my surroundings
- To hide myself behind fulfilling the needs of others
- Keep the peace at any cost
- People please
- Don't make waves
- Don't say how I feel
- Don't be vulnerable
- Avoid conflict
- Avoid confrontation
- AND... REMAIN SILENT

My husband's coping mechanisms from childhood were:

- To not trust
- Emotional and physical withdrawal
- To be hypersensitive to his surroundings
- A need to know everything to have a sense of control
- Anger

- Jealousy
- Mood swings
- Depression
- Diligently be on the lookout for danger
- AND... REQUIRE TOTAL HONESTY AND TRANSPARENCY

My coping mechanism of verbal silence was now in complete opposition to his need for complete truth and honesty at any cost. It was a recipe for disaster.

## Our Journey Together:

The following is a pretty convoluted synopsis of our marriage, but bare with me, and see if you can follow and see the patterns.

I felt as though I lived under a magnifying glass, always being watched for a mis-step that would lead to a confrontational interrogation or a total emotional freezeout. Anytime I would try to take a step forward to better myself, my husband would see it as a threat.

We had many good times, good conversations, intimate moments and shared a child, things that made leaving so hard. But ever-present was his corrosive undercurrent of mistrust and jealousy.

Having both brought children from our previous marriages, and having one together, we found blending a family quite challenging. Our lives revolved around juggling work schedules, children's schedules, step-childrens' visiting schedules, financial burdens, and maintaining a household and relationship, all while carrying our own previously described emotional baggage.

After living this way for 15 years, I reached my first breaking point. It had all become more than I could process and bare. In pure frustration and desperation, I left.

**Break Up #1**

I spent three weeks on my parents' couch, distraught and exhausted. I needed some breathing space, as I had felt as though I was being suffocated. I needed to step out of the story I was living and take a break.

At the end of the three weeks, I drove home to find my husband in the front garden, planting flowers. He had remembered a conversation in which I said that I loved receiving flowers, but they have a limited life span after they are cut. Buying flowers to plant, I thought, seemed to be more environmentally friendly and would be a lasting gift to enjoy over and over again.

As I pulled up, my heart melted. There he was, the man underneath the layers of hurt, pain, frustration, anger, and sadness. There he was, that kind, thoughtful, gentle soul that I fell in love with, giving me what I so greatly needed, to be seen, to be heard, to be loved, to be appreciated, all in one gesture.

I had been filled with a tremendous amount of guilt for leaving. Guilt about breaking up our family and guilt about not being able to hold it all together. Here I was, the self-appointed emotional caretaker of the family, and I was the one that had blown everyone's life apart.

I knew I had to go back and try again.

Things were good for a while upon returning. Both of us were on our best behavior, trying to be mindful not to step on any potential landmine that would blow everything apart again.

But there were many landmines in that household and in our relationship, and as time went by, the cycle began to repeat itself. The patterns were set, and the trajectory would lead to the same outcome. Perhaps with a new catalyst this time, but once again, I found myself at the edge of my ability to keep it all together for everyone's sake and at the edge of my ability to tolerate living this way.

I didn't want to end my relationship. I wanted the pain and suffering to stop for both of us. I wanted the destructive behaviors to stop that were undermining our ability to stay together as a couple and be happy. I was living in a silent hell, torn between staying together, not tearing our family apart, and facing the fear of an unknown future alone.

I remember, on my 33rd birthday, looking out the back bedroom window into our neighbor's yard where they were having a family get-together, with music and laughter, and sobbing as I felt so lonely and so isolated in my pain.

I was living my life walking on eggshells. I had to watch every step, every word, every action, stuffing down the sadness and disappointment I felt. All the while, I was raising three children, dealing with step-children dynamics, and working outside the home at a job that helped to pay the bills, but was so far removed from who I was, that it was sucking the life out of me. A journey I share in my book, *Journal through the Journey of Changing Your Career*.

As my son from my first marriage got older, I could sense the jealousy rising within my husband, and although my son was not aware of this, I was. There was now another strong male presence in the house. My relationship with my own son had become a simmering volcano of jealousy for my husband. I knew this was triggering flashbacks to the revolving males that took his mother's attention away from him as a small boy.

This is how we get triggered in relationships. Our mind takes a present circumstance that feels familiar and reaches back into our childhood and makes a connection. We are not necessarily responding to the present circumstance, but the emotional memory stored in our body.

This happened a lot in our relationship for both of us.

There were so many things that I needed to say, so many behaviors and misperceptions that I needed to confront, but I kept silent to keep the peace. Silence had been my safety, and now my silence was killing me. My fears would not allow me to break open and speak my truth, and my husband was not a safe place to receive it.

We tried going to counseling separately and together. My husband was prescribed an anti-depressant which, in retrospect, only served to numb him rather than allow him to deal with his issues and the issues in our relationship. As a couple, we needed help, and as individuals, we needed to work through our own issues, but to try to do it simultaneously with the life we were living was impossible.

**Break Up #2**

The tension once again escalated. The inner conversation began, "Should I stay? Should I go? Show me a sign. I need help with this. I'm afraid to stay and I'm afraid to leave." The sign came after my husband raged at my son for eating the last piece of pie. The tension, frustration, everything stuffed and unspoken, exploded out of the volcano, and I left again.

This time I stayed away for five months. I was the one to leave the house again, because, quite frankly, although I wanted to leave the relationship, I still stayed in the role of the caretaker for everyone in that household. I knew my husband would have nowhere to go. Even though it had become unbearable for both of us, I was the one who had made the choice to leave. This came again with tremendous guilt, so I displaced myself instead of disrupting the lives of everyone in the house, or so I thought.

It would be our daughter, at 13 years old, who would feel the greatest impact of my decision. She was coming into the rebellious teen years and began spinning out of control.

The guilt for breaking her world apart, and my responsibility as a mother, led me to the very tough decision to move back into the family home to live, not as a couple, but under the same roof in order to help my daughter through these years.

My two older children were living away from home at this point, but my youngest was now on a serious path of self-destructive behavior. I could not leave her and I knew my husband was incapable of handling this on his own. Our difficulties would have to wait.

What I found was that my husband and I got along quite amicably, in fact, quite well when we were not in an intimate relationship. When we were not in the role of "spouse" and all of the implications that go along with that, we were fine. In fact, it was quite enjoyable. None of our buttons were being pushed. There were no expectations, no arguments, and life was good for a while living this way.

But over time, enjoying and relaxing into our platonic life, the attraction naturally increased. Here was the man I loved, the father of my child, and I wanted more. I wanted that missing piece, the closeness, the intimate relationship. Why couldn't we have it all? Weren't all of the pieces right here under this roof? This time, surely, it could be different.

And so, we resumed our spousal relationship. We reunited again for the third time, and even with all of the good intentions brought to it, the cycle, of course, began yet again.

**Break Up #3**

One year later, the relationship collapsed again, and we put the For Sale sign on the lawn to sell our home.

You would think that this would have been our final chapter, but alas, it wasn't.

After our home sold, I had arranged for my daughter and I to live in my friend's one-bedroom basement apartment. Until the closing date, my husband and I again, would live as friends under the same roof, and the problems again disappeared as our friendship refreshed. But, our daughter was still having issues, and between the two of us, my husband and I could not decide what the best thing to do was.

What do I do when I, once again, am blowing my child's life apart? My husband was increasingly stressed from work issues, and as always was relying on me to find a workable solution. The closing date was nearing, and I felt once again responsible for the well-being of everyone else, so I decided that we would all move to my secured one-bedroom basement apartment and go on a trip to see if we could clear the air and push the restart button for all three of us, yet again.

This sounds absolutely insane. I know. But at the time, I could not cope with the horrendous weight and upset at not only ending a relationship but now leaving a home in which I had raised my children. I just couldn't bare the sadness, and the "fixer" in me wanted to alleviate everyone's suffering, including my own.

Something in me was just absolutely unwilling to admit defeat and start all over.

As I look back, I was spinning in a whirl of anger, disappointment, resentment, anxiety, sadness, grief, frustration, and devastation at the loss of a dream and at the impact of my decisions on the people around me. I carried the emotional weight of it all.

Upon returning from our reset vacation, the three of us began living in the tiny basement apartment originally secured for myself and my daughter, and the cycle continued.

We had reunited as a couple again, and after several cramped but contented months, we decided to buy a four-bedroom home, hoping for yet another geographical fresh start of happy family life.

My two older children had been struggling to live on their own, and each took a turn moving back into our new home. But amidst the comings and goings, in hindsight, my making space for everyone, although I enjoyed it, only exacerbated the tension, and the same destructive patterns began to arise as they always had.

**Break Up #4**

Over and over again, the cycle repeated, the inevitable boiling point comes, and instead of breaking my silence and demanding a workable solution, I left again.

I moved into a friend's home where I lived for three months, and due to the pressure from my friend to reunite and work on my relationship, I moved back in with my husband.

This time, we added a new ingredient. Although I have referred to my "husband" throughout this story, it was not until we moved into this home, now 18 years into our relationship, that we decided to officially get married. Perhaps this was the glue that would bind us together forever. Perhaps this was the security that was needed, the sign of love and devotion that would put to rest all of our insecurities.

We had a wedding ceremony at home surrounded by family and friends, and left in the early hours for the airport to go on our honeymoon, a cruise to the Virgin Islands. We were having a lovely time, but then, at dinner halfway through our cruise, I could see the familiar dark shadow cross my husband's face. I knew he was sinking into that place where I would be emotionally abandoned, shut out, and left wondering what I had said or done. I never knew what his mind was chewing on and I was always far too frozen in fear to confront it. My silence always met his darkness, hoping it would pass.

The next day I spent alone on my honeymoon. My heart sank as I walked back to the room. But even though I was glad to see that his mood had lifted, and we were fine for the rest of the trip, I knew in my heart that marriage had fixed nothing.

The patterns continued when we arrived back home. But worse, there was another issue we were faced with. Our now 18-year-old daughter was pregnant. I share this journey in *Journal Through the Journey of Accepting Your Child's Journey.*

I knew in my heart that I had raised my three children, and I was not prepared to raise another, so the decision was made to move my daughter into an apartment with my son, and we were back to an empty nest. We decided we no longer needed or wanted a four-bedroom home, so we downsized and moved into a condo.

This would be our final home together.

We renovated well together; I had the vision, and he had the ability to create it. It was a project that kept us busy and focused on working together. But the issues that lay beneath the surface would inevitably surface at some point. And they did.

My husband required total honesty and transparency. I knew this, but it was also my experience with him that anything that I said could and would be used against me at a later date. He had a brilliant mind that would remember every single detail and an ability to pull information stored in a moment when he needed it. I, on the other hand, became flustered with confrontation, and my mind would go blank. I would need time to think, digest, and respond. My husband saw this as withholding and saw this as being deceitful. Flashback to age seven, when his mother withheld important information about his eye surgery that caused him trauma.

Having been fallaciously treated as a small child to the point of trauma, my husband had grown from a lied-to child into a brilliant grown man with a self-justified inability to sense personal boundaries within himself or for others closest to him.

Unknown to me at the time, he had been reading my personal journals and would test me with questions to see what I would answer. His inability to trust led him to try to piece circumstances together to prove this theory of my untrustworthiness. This led him to tape conversations, read my emails, and go through my computer to monitor the websites I was looking at, always in search of evidence to find me guilty.

My husband inherently did not believe that he was worthy of love or that I would stay with him, and he spent most of our married life trying to prove this to be true. Instead of focusing on being the man I so desperately wanted, he spent most of his time pushing me away, thus creating a self-fulfilling prophecy of abandonment.

I contributed to his mistrust by not having the courage and ability to stand up and say exactly how I felt, to push back, to back myself up, to say what I needed to say no matter what. And there it was, the irreconcilable difference that would be the demise of our relationship. He needed the security of complete honesty, and feeling unsafe being my default, my security lay in the self-protection of silence.

One evening, my husband was in what I would refer to as "his mood". This is where he sat in a chair silently brooding and not talking to me. This always triggered a response in me to question: What had I done? What did I say? It was an emotional stonewalling that happened quite frequently in our relationship and left me feeling emotionally disconnected, unloved, and alone—a familiar feeling from my childhood.

I had learned to not go into that dark cave after him or question him, as whatever was swirling around his psyche would inevitably come at me with a vengeance regardless of my demeanor or intention.

This particular evening, he was in his dark cave, shutting me out, so I had gone to bed to read, hoping that his darkness would lift. As I lay in bed, I received a text from my daughter's boyfriend asking if I could loan him $40.

I lay there thinking to myself that my interacting with other men was a hot button for my husband, no matter who they were, and now I could feel a familiar knot forming in my stomach as I sensed the implications of this scenario.

I knew withholding this information from my husband would trigger him at some point and again I would be deemed untrustworthy, but at the same time, I also knew I wanted to have some power to help. Things needed to change, as I was, once again, in a no-win situation.

I pushed back the covers, and naked, I got out of bed and began down the hall towards the living room. I acknowledged the emotional nakedness and vulnerability I was feeling inside as I was about to enter his cave, somehow hoping this would show him my sincerity and honest desire to address this issue together.

I walked towards my husband, trying to read the energy in the room and on his face, and I slowly lowered myself down onto his lap. He was allowing this, which gave me hope, as I was trying ever so delicately to lift him out of the darkness. I reached my arms around him and gave him a hug, telling myself that it would be ok, and he seemed to be open. I then told him that I had just received a text from our daughter's boyfriend, asking if I could loan him $40.

My husband paused for a moment, and then erupted at me in anger and disgust, "Get Off, Just Get Off Me," as he pushed my naked body off of his lap. The intensity of his rage slashed my heart into a million pieces, his words reaching in and ripping at my flesh. I had stepped on a landmine, my heart, my soul, my hope, all torn apart in a moment.

I felt I had done nothing wrong and had attempted at my very core to give him what he asked for, truth and transparency, and in doing so, I had been evisorated. I slowly turned away from him, humiliated, horrified, and holding it all in as I always did, composing myself to walk away with as much dignity as I could muster. I quietly mouthed the words, "NEVER AGAIN."

I shrank back down the hallway, trying to hold back my tears, crawled back into bed, and raised the covers to somehow comfort and cover what I had just experienced, but my heart sank even deeper as I heard his coarse footsteps coming down the hall towards me.

He stood over me and began berating me for approaching him when he was in a bad mood. I did not hear most of what he said at that point as I had left my body, sending his words fading into the background where they could no longer hurt me. I watched in horror as his face morphed into that of an 84-year-old man, revealing the devastating truth that I would need to surrender to: if I stayed, this would continue to be my life to the end.

It was in this moment that a voice rose up inside of me, a voice that had been silent for our entire marriage, a voice that rose above everything, including my fear of being alone, and it said, as clear as a bell, "NO MORE."

**Break Up #5 The Final Straw**

My relationship was truly over, and in that moment, I knew it. I would need to face my fear of being alone. I needed to have the inner strength and courage to embark on a journey after hearing my truth resound within me, and that is exactly what I did. After a sleepless night, I spoke those five words the next day, that would empower me and change the trajectory of my life. I said to my husband, "*I need you to leave.*"

Finally, after years of taking care of everyone else's needs and putting my own needs on the back burner, after many attempts to resurrect a marriage and life from the ashes, I came to a grinding halt. I could no longer live in this cycle of destruction and devastation. I needed it all to stop. I needed to close the door, and in doing so, open myself up to the possibilities of a new chapter. My life needed to change, and no matter what, I could not turn back. I share this journey in *Journal Through the Journey of Letting Go of Your Home.*

**My Reflection:** *The journey to this final decision was an incredibly hard and long one. I had desired with all my heart for this relationship to work, but desire alone would not get us there. There was much inner work for both of us to do, and we would need to do it separately. I was going to need the courage to embark on my solitary journey, face my fear of being alone, and build within myself the strength and ability to create the life I desired. Here's the thing I had to learn. My husband and I were not broken, we were two people carrying the wounds of childhood trauma who had inadvertently created layer upon layer of coping mechanisms that would deem us unable to successfully live together as a healthy whole. Underneath all of these layers, I was whole. Time alone does not heal. I needed to fill this time with doing the work necessary to remove what was blocking me from knowing and experiencing this.*

## Your Journey Continues:

1.  Describe where you are at in the ending of your relationship

2.  What do you need to let go of in order to have the life you desire?

3.  What fears keep you from making a decision?

4.  How will your life change if you stay or if you go?

5.  Describe any irreconcilable differences you have/had.

6.  How does it feel to face into a future alone?

7.  How will ending your relationship impact those around you?

8.  What was/is your deciding factor?

9.  What support do you have in place for making a decision?

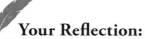

## Your Reflection:

Having allowed some time to pass since working with the prompts and re-reading your responses, ask yourself:

What stands out for me is ........................................................

The recurring patterns I can see are ........................................

My learning is ......................................................................

My next step will be ...........................................................

# FACETS
# OF THE
# JOURNEY

# MY SILENCE

*"There is much to explore in the silence."*

## My Journey:

It had been my experience growing up that words carried a lot of power and had the ability to lift me up or hurt me very deeply. My father's own wounded spirit, made it his nature to ridicule, criticize, demean, deflate dreams, and tear down any sense of my self-worth. The words that were spoken and the words that were not spoken in my home changed who I was and who I could become. I could never counter my father's words, there was no space for my voice, and so they remained deep inside of me.

My silence was a learned coping mechanism, a way to step into the background for security and for safety. There was helplessness and hopelessness attached to my silence. It was a place of resignation to the reality that I did not feel safe in my environment, and I was powerless as a child to change it.

I can recall a very heated argument between my parents around the age of four when my mother was enraged at my father and slapped him in the face. Her anger scared me, and I turned and ran upstairs, crying, saying to myself that I would always just agree, not make any waves, just go along to keep the peace. The trajectory of a pattern of silence and fear of anger and confrontation was set, and this is what I brought into my relationships.

When you have no safe place as a child, no adult to listen to you, to acknowledge what you are saying, when you feel as though you are insignificant, then you are left with your own small voice trying to make sense of the world and your significance in it. You have no understanding or language for your experience. You are left alone, with no words.

Flash forward to the conflicts within my marriage, I had to take an honest look at my inability to fight back, to say how I was feeling, to speak my truth.

Why did I not speak my truth?

- Speaking my truth had a lot of implications for a lot of people.
- Speaking my truth meant that there would be constant arguing in the house and I did not want my children to be exposed to a volatile environment.
- Speaking my truth potentially meant turning my and my children's lives upside down.
- Speaking my truth, once spoken, could not be reversed. It was out there, and that would mean change.
- Speaking my truth meant being vulnerable, opening myself up to hurt, pain, abandonment, loneliness, poverty, angst, and depression,
- Speaking my truth would mean selling the home and being a single parent of three small children.
- Speaking my truth meant hurting my spouse.
- Speaking my truth meant being seen.
- Speaking my truth meant letting go of my dream of the loving family unit that I had always desired. The spouse, the children, and the home were the key ingredients in my vision of happiness and fulfillment.

- Speaking my truth meant setting myself up for what always felt like a full-on battle regarding my entire adult life, as my past mistakes prior to our relationship would always be used against me.

My nervous system, my coping mechanisms, and my perceived ability to deal with the repercussions of speaking my truth were not strong enough. My confidence was not strong enough, and although I tried to convey my truth at times, it was always dismissed as an excuse. I had nowhere to go. I always felt like my words had no power.

They say actions speak louder than words. But in my experience, silence was an action as well. Silence was the action I took to keep my family together, to keep a marriage intact, to keep it all together, until my silence was killing me.

**My Reflection:** *My silence on the outside, did not translate to silence on the inside. On the inside, it was a totally different story. This is where I was holding all of the hurt, pain, disappointment, and unspoken words that were accumulating over the years. On the inside, my mind, my heart, my organs, cells, and tissues, were all carrying the heavy weight of my lived experience that would eventually take a toll.*

## Your Journey:

1.  Where in your life are you silent?

2.  What are the implications of speaking your truth?

3.  What longs to be spoken?

4.  How has silence helped or hindered your relationships?

5.  Describe how speaking your truth has been received.

6.  What holds you back from speaking your truth?

7.  Where can you go in your life to speak your truth?

8.  What do you need to be able to speak your truth?

9.  Describe the ramifications of not speaking your truth.

 **Your Reflection:**

Having allowed some time to pass since working with the prompts and re-reading your responses, ask yourself:

What stands out for me is ......................................................

The recurring patterns I can see are ...................................

My learning is ...............................................................

My next step will be ......................................................

# BELIEFS

*"Check underneath the hood of your beliefs."*

## My Journey:

Beliefs are formed by our experiences and our interpretation of these experiences, as well as societal, familial, and generational programming. There were fundamental beliefs that were at play in our relationship that would contribute to its demise. We were not seeing the truth, we were each seeing our own interpretation of the truth, according to our individual lived experiences so far. We were living out our unconscious programming, unable to see what the real issues were that were running and ruining our relationship.

In the middle of most be**lie**fs is a "lie". Beliefs are rarely challenged, but hold the key to some of the choices and behaviors that hinder us from living in our success.

I had to take a look at what I believed, not in my mind, not what I wanted to believe, but in my actions and reactions. What were they telling me, not about my husband, but about myself? What was I really bringing into this relationship? It would be easy to point the finger at my husband and declare him the "problem," but this was my second failed marriage, and the common denominator was me. I needed to take a good look at my part, take responsibility, and do the inner work to make some fundamental changes, because if I didn't, no matter what relationship I was in, history would repeat itself.

I came up with several beliefs to challenge as a starting point, and began to write. I invite you to answer these as well, or come up with your own beliefs to hold up, examine, and question. After each limiting belief, I then wrote out an affirmation to counter this belief.

## What did I believe about men?

**Limiting Belief:**

My experience with men in my formative years included alcoholism, betrayal, sexual abuse, and emotional negligence. My search for love began at a very young age, as I decided that I would need to look outside of my home for love and validation. I saw men as holding the key to my happiness, the determiners of my loveability, the judgers of my worthiness, and the keepers of my heart, and yet at the same time, I did not like them very much. In my experience, they hurt me, disappointed me, and were not trustworthy. They used me for their own gratification, and held me in little regard. As I write this, I'm thinking to myself, "How in the world did I think I would ever be able to have a healthy intimate relationship with this core belief about men?"

**Affirmation:**

*A partner is a compliment to my life, not a reason or a necessity for my life. I am ok on my own, and reinforcing this core belief empowers me to have a healthy relationship if that is what I choose.*

## What did I believe about intimacy?

**Limiting Belief:**

I had no frame of reference for intimacy. I don't think I even understood what it looked like or meant. There were no moments of connection in conversation in my family. There was no heart-to-heart sharing, there was no healthy role modeling of a loving relationship. As far as sexual intimacy, upon entering my adolescent years, my first sexual experience was that of abuse by an adult over an extended period of time. Intimacy would also mean that I would need to trust and be vulnerable, and with a trauma-infused childhood, that was impossible for me.

**Affirmation:**

*I break down the walls I have built around my heart. If I am strong within myself, then I will be strong and safe within the relationship of my choosing.*

## Was I capable of trust?

**Limiting Belief:**

As a young person, there was no safe place, no adult to confide in or take me under their wing. Trust was a concept and a hope, but not a belief. In my experience, the world was not to be trusted. I remember thinking as an adolescent that I did not like the adult world. It seemed to be full of lies, deceit, and heartbreak.

**Affirmation:**

*I trust me. I trust my judgement. I trust my intuition. I can have the boundaries within myself to let go and know when it is safe to trust.*

*People will hurt me, and I will hurt them. It is human nature, but I trust I will come through intact.*

## What did I believe about relationships?

### Limiting Belief:

I wanted to believe that relationships held the possibility for deep connection, deep honesty, intimacy, and a shared life experience. I wanted that to be true, but relationships for me were disjointed, void of deep connection, or communication, and a place in which I could not insert myself very well without all of my buttons being pushed. Being in a relationship required me to call upon tools that I had not developed. I had no idea how to connect in a healthy way to another human being. I would repeat the familiar pattern of my family of origin, four people living under one roof, swirling around in their own pain with little to no connection.

### Affirmation:

*I deserve healthy, whole, intimate relationships in all facets of my life. I will use my voice, speak my truth, and be valued in all of my relationships.*

## What did I believe about my own worthiness of love?

**Limiting Belief:**

Deep down inside, I did not feel worthy of love. I desired it, I searched for it, but fundamentally, I did not feel worthy of it. I had looked outside of myself and put my worth in the hands of other people. In bringing this into a relationship, I also brought in heaps of insecurity, as at any moment in time, my partner could withdraw their love, which I would interpret as proof of my unworthiness.

**Affirmation:**

*I have an incredible ability to feel love, and I know that as I love and value myself, a love that is worthy of me will appear.*

## What did I believe about honesty?

**Limiting Belief:**

Honesty meant vulnerability. Honesty meant setting myself up for rejection, abandonment, and withdrawal of love. It represented the possibility and probability of conflict, being seen and heard. Honesty would require that I had the ability to cope with its consequences and outcomes, when I fundamentally didn't believe that I did.

**Affirmation:**

*I must be honest with myself and with others, with courage. I owe this to myself. Sometimes honesty will bring conflict, and that's ok because the integrity of myself and my life is worth fighting for.*

Through my journaling, I finally began to see and link the demise of my relationship to the experiences of my past, my created coping mechanisms, and the role model of my parents' broken relationship. All these together had left me completely unable to have a healthy intimate relationship.

If I hung onto these limiting beliefs about myself, about men, and about intimate relationships, I would keep repeating the same cycle. If I hung onto limiting beliefs about myself and my lack of worthiness, if I did not find my voice, then again, I would keep repeating the same cycle.

I had to uncover and hold up each limiting belief to examine where it came from, where it was hindering me, and ask myself if it was, in fact, true, and was I honestly willing and able to let it go.

Letting it go did not take one decision and then it was gone. These beliefs were infused into who I was. I was going to need to be diligently mindful and conscious of the beliefs that were driving my thoughts, words, choices, and actions. I would need to be aware of the lens that I was looking through at any given moment.

If my beliefs were to change, it would take time to practice changing the inner programming that had been running in the background for most of my life.

I was also aware that if I just believed that I had chosen the "wrong" man, then I would continue putting the onus of responsibility outside of myself onto someone else. If I stayed in a state of blaming my childhood, blaming my parents, blaming society, and always looking outside of myself as the "problem," then nothing would change.

I had spent many years trying to control my outer environment so that I would feel ok. What I have come to know is that feeling ok on the inside no matter what is happening on the outside, and a belief that no matter what happens, I will be ok, is what see's me through the challenging times.

**My Reflection:** *It is in the taking of responsibility for my life, for my happiness, for my desired outcomes, and the belief in my ability to change that leads to my success. If I do not believe in my worthiness to have the life I desire, there is no where to go. I will sabotage my efforts and live out a self-fulfilling prophecy and have regret.*

 **Your Reflection:**

1. Write out a list of the limiting beliefs that are impacting your ability to have the life you desire.

2. Where did you learn these beliefs?

3. What beliefs are negatively impacting your relationship?

4. How will changing your beliefs change your desired outcome?

5. What beliefs do you need to let go of?

6. Describe how your limiting beliefs are showing up in your actions.

7. Write out the limiting beliefs you came up with in #1 and beside each, write out an affirmation to counter each belief that will help to move you forward.

8. How would it feel in your body to let go of limiting beliefs?

9. What does taking responsibility for your happiness look like for you?

## Your Reflection:

Having allowed some time to pass since working with the prompts and re-reading your responses, ask yourself:

What stands out for me is ......................................................

The recurring patterns I can see are ........................................

My learning is ...................................................................

My next step will be ..........................................................

# FEAR OF BEING ALONE

*"Courage will lead the way through your fears."*

## My Journey:

While my silence was one of my biggest coping mechanisms, my fear of being alone was the fear that was also driving many of my choices and decisions. I had lived my life as a chameleon, always scanning my environment to see who I needed to be, as well as needing other people to define who I was.

Within our relationship, I had a role, I had a purpose, I had significance, and I was a part of something, and that is what I desired the most, to belong.

I did not want, nor did I know how to be on my own. To be alone, there would be no one to love me, to roll over and talk to in bed. There would be no one to emotionally lean on, to bounce ideas off of. There would be no one to plan a future with. I would be no one's person, and belong to no one. It felt as though I would not exist.

The prospect of being by myself, felt like death to me, as I was not centered in a healthy sense of self, with high self worth and esteem. I had no proven self-efficacy or self-reliance in my back pocket, so I put the onus on my husband to give me significance.

The fear of being alone kept me silent. It made me turn a blind eye and not address unacceptable behavior. It kept me silent instead of doing what I really wanted to do, which was to fight back. This fear had a firm grip on me throughout our relationship, as the possible consequences of speaking my truth would be too high.

I perceived that being on my own would mean that I had failed. It would be proof that I was incapable and unworthy of having a successful intimate relationship. It would prove that I was unlovable.

What I hadn't realized was that I was already alone. I was alone inside of myself, and I was alone in the relationship. If I could not bring the truth of who I was and what I was thinking and feeling, then my husband was not even having a relationship with me. He was having a relationship with an untrue version of me, a version of myself that would do and be anything to not be by myself.

As I journaled my way through to this deeper understanding, I started to make room for the possibility that for me to speak my truth, I was going to need to know who I was. I was going to need to get acquainted with a part of myself that I had continually pushed down and silenced all of these years.

I was going to need to face my fears in order to overcome them. If I did not face them and understand them, then I would be doomed under their influence for the rest of my life. I needed to let the real Linda step forward and take charge.

I would also need to rethink my perception of being alone and the negative connotation I had attached to it. I needed to empower myself to see that alone time was, in fact, exactly what I needed. I needed to become my own safe place to fall, my own rock, my own best friend and confidant.

There were no big gaps between relationships in my life. I shifted from relationship to relationship with very little time in between to pause and spend time with myself, to build a sense of self-reliance, to know that I could cope with whatever challenges I experienced. I had not as yet built that muscle, a muscle I would need to develop to live the life I desired to live.

Living successfully on my own would give me the independence and lived experience of self reliance. It would give me the inner strength to speak my truth no matter what. This is what I would need in order to have success.

**My Reflection:** *My fear of being alone was the stone that needed to be overturned and examined. I had to understand the implications for my life if I hung onto this fear. I would not be able to move forward, and I would continue to repeat the same pattern in future relationships. I needed to be comfortable with my own company, develop interests, and create a life centered around who I was. I needed to move through the fear to feel the freedom on the other side of it.*

## Your Journey:

1. Describe how the fear of being alone impacts your choices and decisions.

2. How has the fear of being alone kept you silent or disempowered?

3. What does being alone look like for you?

4. How does/did the fear of being alone impact your relationship?

5. What do you need to let go of in order to be ok with being alone?

6. What do you need to happen to overcome your fear of being alone?

7. Describe your sense of self-worth and self-efficacy.

8. In what ways has your dependency on your partner affected your relationship?

9. How would you feel in your body if you were not in a relationship?

## Your Reflection:

Having allowed some time to pass since working with the prompts and re-reading your responses, ask yourself:

What stands out for me is ......................................................

The recurring patterns I can see are ........................................

My learning is ......................................................

My next step will be ......................................................

# PATTERNS AND COPING MECHANISMS

*"Break the ties that bind you that stand in the way of your freedom."*

## My Journey:

We had hit an impasse and the one thing I knew for sure was that my husband and I were in a cycle of suffering that could only be stopped by ending our marital relationship. The toxic dynamic of each of our patterns and coping mechanisms were not fixable within our relationship.

Interestingly, though, in those times when my husband and I were not in the role of spouse to one another, we got along great. This also was a pattern for us. There had been no tension, no arguments, no emotional withdrawal, every coping mechanism fell away. This had been an integral part of our relationship cycle, and one that I needed to acknowledge and explore further.

When we were in the role of spouse to one another we had something to lose. When we were in the role of spouse, we were recreating our family of origin story. My husband in his dire need for love, acknowledgment and acceptance from his mother, and his history of being abandoned and betrayed by her, imprinted within him a subconscious belief that love was a double-edged sword. He longed to be loved, but also believed that he would be destroyed by it. He was always on the lookout for when the shoe would drop, and when the woman he loved would abandon him. This subconscious belief led him to be hypervigilant in monitoring his environment, and me, for the threat that he believed would inevitably appear and ultimately leave him, once again all alone.

For me, coming from a place of feeling unlovable, unworthy of love, and living in an environment where the negative imprints of alcoholism, judgment, and criticism were experienced on a regular basis, my coping mechanism was to hide, remain silent and invisible, to not be vulnerable and to always scan my environment for potential danger. As a child, I was not able to physically leave my home, but what I was able to do was to leave mentally and emotionally. I learned to hide inside of myself and disconnect from the outside world. This created in me, as an adult, the impulse to either run or hide or both, never to stay, to be vulnerable and speak my truth.

In both of our cases, our initial experiences of love, family, and connection had been broken and were severely impacting our ability to have a healthy attachment to one another.

Our subconscious had stored our experiences and made the connection, that family equals pain, and conflict, and is not a safe place. When we would break up, we removed the "family" pattern buried beneath our awareness and all would be well.

When we were not in a relationship, there was no fear of loss, no expectations put on each other, we could relax and not be on guard, or on the lookout for possible danger to our well-being.

In our friendship cycle, our fears and insecurities were not running the show. We were unburdened, and untriggered, and things were peaceful. All the qualities that I loved about my husband emerged as his heart and psyche were no longer under the constant threat of his perceived fear of abandonment and I could speak my truth without consequence.

We were, and always would be, connected, as we continued to co-parent, so ties could never be completely severed. This ongoing connection would inevitably lead to spending time together, feeling comfortable with one another, and then a longing for something more would rise up, beginning our doomed cycle once again as we would attempt to live as husband and wife.

I had to identify my own patterns and coping mechanisms to see how they were contributing to the breakdown of our relationship and who I was as a person. Knowing myself became really important to understand my reactions, behavior, and choices. I used my journal to become the observer of myself and to identify unhealthy thoughts, perceptions, and behaviors that were detrimental to me having the loving, intimate relationship I desired.

I discovered, deep within, my learned state of being in "want". I *wanted* a loving, nurturing family of origin, I *wanted* a loving, intimate relationship with my spouse. My focus was always from a place of lack and wanting. I did not have the tools within me to "create and have" only to "want." I was incapable of acknowledging, receiving and sustaining the love I so desperately "wanted".

I can remember with my first husband, I was in "pursuit" mode. I was in the "want" phase, and when we finally came together as a couple, it was like a switch turned off inside of me. A shift in perception that I did not understand at that time, but what was a beautiful beginning turned into angst inside of me. I was now confronted with all of my insecurities, unhealthy thinking, and perceptions, and it became unbearable. A short four-year marriage and two children later, I could not handle the buttons that were being pushed inside of me, and I fled, unable to receive the love I was being offered.

I needed to recognize the patterns and cycles I was in and work to let go of what was no longer serving me or my relationships.

My cycle:

- I did not feel lovable, so I would look outside of myself for love and validation
- I would resort to my ingrained patterns and coping mechanisms
- I was unable to define or communicate my needs
- I would leave mentally, emotionally, or physically.
- I did not feel worthy as a person, so I put my worth in someone else's hands

## MY TOXIC RELATIONSHIP CYCLE

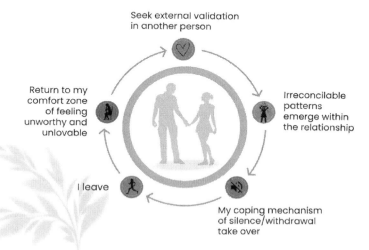

Seek external validation in another person

Irreconcilable patterns emerge within the relationship

My coping mechanism of silence/withdrawal take over

I leave

Return to my comfort zone of feeling unworthy and unlovable

Finally recognizing and understanding my patterns and coping mechanism cycles empowered me to make changes. With awareness, I could think differently and act differently. I could make conscious choices to empower myself that would, over time, trickle into my subconscious and replace everything that was holding me back. But I could not accomplish this for myself within my relationship, so I broke the cycle that was trapping me in such fundamental ways.

**My Reflection:** *I believed in my subconscious that I was unworthy of having a healthy, intimate relationship, and so did my husband. Together with our inner patterns and coping mechanisms in full unconscious swing, that is exactly what we created.*

## Your Journey:

1.  Identify the unhealthy patterns that you see manifesting in your relationship.

2.  Identify the coping mechanisms that are blocking you from being who you want to be in the relationship.

3. Describe where these patterns and coping mechanisms originated.

4. Write a positive affirmation beside each unhealthy pattern and coping mechanism.

5. What does ending these patterns and cycles look like for you?

6. What does your life look like if you do not end these patterns and cycles?

7. How will changing your perspective change your relationship with yourself?

8. What do you need to do to feel empowered within yourself?

9. What do you need to let go of, or develop within yourself to have the relationship you desire?

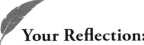

## Your Reflection:

Having allowed some time to pass since working with the prompts and re-reading your responses, ask yourself:

What stands out for me is ......................................................

The recurring patterns I can see are .........................................

My learning is ................................................................

My next step will be ...........................................................

# BOUNDARIES

*"To thine own self be true."*

William Shakespeare

## My Journey:

Growing up in an emotionally dysfunctional family, I had learned to attune myself to the needs and feelings of my parents rather than the other way around. As I grew up and into adulthood, this translated into my not developing a clear sense of self and boundaries. The needs of those around me always trumped what I was feeling inside because I had never had an audience for my emotional needs. I did not develop healthy personal boundaries because I never felt like I actually existed. In fact, my boundaries were merely a combination of either defaulting to the boundaries of others, or rigidly closing myself off so no one could get in, either physically or emotionally.

The needs of the many outweighed the needs of the one. My needs never mattered to anyone, not even myself. My purpose became to identify, acquiesce or fix for others, regardless of the consequences to myself.

This led to developing a strong "fixer" personality trait. I believed that to feel safe and secure, I would need to be responsible for everything and everyone in my external environment. If everyone outside of myself was ok, then I was too. I placed a low priority on my own needs in exchange for an illusion of safety. My needs were always last, or non-existent therefore I never developed any degree of self-sufficiency or autonomy. I was codependent on the people around me to define my worth and purpose because basically I had learned to not count.

When you don't have an established sense of self or self-worth, there is no standing up for yourself because essentially you don't count or exist. You are an extension of those around you. You have no sense of your own likes and dislikes, so you take on the likes and dislikes of those around you. You bend and contort yourself to find your significance in meeting the needs of others. This is how I existed for many years.

Boundaries, as defined by www.dictionary.cambridge.org, state that "a boundary is a real or imagined line that marks the edge or limit of something." Because I had never been given or given myself an opportunity to explore who I truly was beyond the role of servicing the needs of others, I had never defined a clear set of personal values that would have required healthy boundaries to be implemented and enforced.

I would either merge with your needs and boundaries or would shut you out altogether. Either way, I created a state of deep inner loneliness and isolation, and essentially felt like a walking open wound most of the time, always dependant on the wellbeing of those around me.

Healthy boundaries help to define what is appropriate and what is inappropriate. My need to be loved overshadowed any sense of violation of personal boundaries. And though I felt the sting, I remained silent.

My husband also had no personal boundaries, which for him, translated into searching through my journals, taping my conversations, reading emails, and checking my browser histories to suss out ways I was going to betray him.

In both cases, we put our broken sense of worth, purpose, and happiness in each other's hands, and in doing so, we were destined to destroy the relationship.

Establishing autonomy for myself would mean that I needed to turn my focus inwards to create a new solid foundation within myself, a foundation of worthiness, self-love, self-acceptance, and self-sufficiency regardless of all things external. It was a monumental sense of self-responsibility that would ultimately empower me to be the woman I have become today.

I am still able to offer help to those around me but now it is at my discretion and on my terms. My boundaries are clearly defined and they matter a great deal to my health and wellness.

**My Reflection:** *Healthy boundaries would mean that I didn't have to constantly do for others at the expense of myself. I could say yes when I wanted to and no when I didn't want to do something. I would empower myself by experiencing that the world would not fall apart if I said no. Healthy boundaries meant spending time cultivating a relationship with myself, really getting to know what I valued, and then having the boundaries to honor those values.*

# Your Journey:

1.  Identify how a lack of boundaries is impacting your relationship.

2.  Where in your life do you need more personal boundaries?

3.  Describe what personal boundaries look like for you.

4.  Define what you value in yourself and in your relationship.

5.  How would setting boundaries affect all of your relationships?

6.  What stops you from setting boundaries?

7.  Describe what autonomy looks and feels like for you.

8. How can you honor yourself in your relationships?

9. Where do you say yes when you want to say no and how does this make you feel?

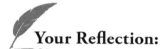 **Your Reflection:**

Having allowed some time to pass since working with the prompts and re-reading your responses, ask yourself:

What stands out for me is .....................................................

The recurring patterns I can see are .........................................

My learning is .................................................................

My next step will be ..........................................................

# FAIRYTALES &
# WHITE PICKET
# FENCES

*"Explore beyond the known."*

## My Journey:

"Happily ever after" was a dangling carrot I had been chasing. The main narrative I was following was: go to school, find someone to love, get married, work at a great job, buy a home with a white picket fence, have children, and live happily ever after. That was the program.

I can remember when I met my first husband, I wanted to leave my tumultuous childhood behind and step into a new chapter in adulthood. I had ticked all of the boxes, and followed the program exactly as prescribed. I had the guy, the job, the home, and two children, and it all fell apart.

The second time around, I tried again, I had the guy, the job, the home, and now three children, and it all fell apart. Let me state here that my two husbands were really great, responsible men. I had not "chosen wrong".

I had to look at my expectations, my desires, and my ability to achieve my vision. I had thought that I had all of the pieces, but with me being the common denominator in both failed marriages, I had to take an honest look at myself and what I was bringing into a relationship.

I knew how to acquire and create the pieces, but I had no ability to assemble them, like doing a puzzle without having the picture on the box. I had never been taught what a happy life and marriage looked like.

The white picket fence, for me, was an external representation of success. It represented that I had happily landed in adulthood and had all of the ingredients for a fulfilling life. In retrospect, I had wanted this so much because inside I felt so broken, that it would prove that I was ok, I was lovable, and I was worthy. I could step out of my past unscathed and just move forward and have a good life.

This was a massive need and expectation to put on a partner, a marriage, and on myself. I was trying to set up my life to look successful on the outside, when what I needed was to work on healing myself on the inside.

I could make my outer world look quite beautiful, but when I would plug myself into the equation, something went askew. I did not have the white picket fence within me. I had the vision and the desire, but I did not have the necessary ingredients to sustain it all.

You can't run away from your past. At some point, you are forced to stop, turn around and face it head on, otherwise you will be chased by these ghosts forever.

*Happily ever after*, is a fairytale life that we read about as little girls, with Sleeping Beauty needing Prince Charming to save the day. This is what was in my psyche. This is what was in my heart. But what I would come to realize over time, was that *I* was Sleeping Beauty, asleep in my own life, and that Prince Charming would be my own consciousness trying to wake me up. To show up for myself, heal myself, love myself, and place my self-worth in my own hands was the consciousness I'd been waiting for my whole life.

I had this vision of myself with all of my needs packed in suitcases and bringing them to my husband in our new home, unpacking each of them and handing them to him with the expectation that he would be responsible for cleaning up this mess. This was not a conscious expectation in my marriage, but it had definitely been implied.

Now I know that my happily ever after is my responsibility. Life has its ups and downs, challenges, and heartbreaks, but the onus is on me to take responsibility for my life and for my happiness. I will never outsource my happiness to a fable ever again.

My version of the white picket fence had held me captive behind its gate. I had become a prisoner of my need to have it all look good from the outside and my need for validation within a relationship. There was much suffering within the confines of my fence and within my mind. I had to know what was beyond the gate of the dilapidated fence, what I could create for myself beyond all of the suffering.

In my efforts to keep all the balls in the air for everyone else in my life and to keep my distorted version of the white picket fence alive, I had lost sight of my dream of being an author and a life coach. But, how could I possibly help anyone else until I had done the work myself?

In spite of everything, I had completed all the training, acquired all of the credentials, and desperately wanted this chapter of my life to take hold, but I had never allowed myself the time, space, or energy to bring this dream into fruition. I needed to open that gate and release myself to grow from the inside out, and most of all, leave all the ghosts of my past behind.

My revised version of my fairytale and white picket fences requires me to take all of my experiences and weave them into a story of triumph. One that will help others on their journey.

**My Reflection:** *My vision of a white picket fence has changed, as has my interpretation of fairytales. I can have what I desire, but that representation of a warm, love-filled sanctuary now comes from within. I now embody the white picket fence, I am my own hero. I decide what gets let in and what needs to go. And if one of the pickets surrounding my sanctuary gets worn or broken, I figure out how to fix it myself, the way I want it to be.*

## Your Journey:

1. What metaphor does the white picket fence represent for you?

2. How have fairytales influenced your perception of relationships?

3. How have unrealistic expectations impacted your relationships?

4. What has caused disappointment in relationships for you?

5. Where can you be your own hero in your life?

6. What does being your own hero require of you?

7. What illusion of happiness do you need to let go of?

8. Describe your ideal relationship.

9. How can you give yourself what you need?

## Your Reflection:

Having allowed some time to pass since working with the prompts and re-reading your responses, ask yourself:

What stands out for me is .......................................................

The recurring patterns I can see are ..........................................

My learning is ...................................................................

My next step will be ............................................................

# NEED VS WANT

*"Follow your heart's desire."*

## My Journey:

There were needs stemming from my broken past that were driving my perceptions and my choices, needs that I was looking outside of myself to be fulfilled. This is where I had to stop and take a good look at my expectations within an intimate relationship and determine where the need was coming from and my own ability to fulfill it.

If I desired to be in an intimate relationship in the future, I would need to heal the wounds that sent me in search of validation, love, and acceptance in the arms of men.

There are personal needs and then there are the needs required for a healthy relationship. Our needs were based in our unhealed childhood experiences. We all have a need for love and connection, but for me, what was attached to that was validation, significance, worth, belonging, and when you put this in someone else's hands, you put great pressure on your partner to fulfill this.

In retrospect, what happened for us was that we took on the roles of being what we thought each other needed, but ultimately, we set ourselves up for failure because at any moment, one mis-step by either of us would rip it all away. In the end, we would be left alone with our original feelings of insignificance, unlovability, and worthlessness. This was the cycle that had to be broken for each of us, but it was impossible to do this together.

Our expectations of one another were unrealistic and fear based, and this does not create a solid foundation on which to build a healthy relationship. We both loved each other, but our love was so weighed down by such debilitating fears that it was not enough.

What I needed was room to grow, a safe, secure environment to be who I was, flaws and all. I needed love and acceptance, and the freedom to be me. With the combination of his insecurities and mine, I morphed myself into what I thought I had to be, what my husband needed me to be, and in the process, I silenced myself, I lost myself, and I became very resentful.

My journey alone would be to address the needs and expectations I was placing outside of myself, and begin giving myself what I needed. In doing this, a future partner would come from a *want* rather than a *need*, a nice to have, rather than a have to have.

In meeting my own needs, I would place the responsibility for my happiness in my own hands. I would be self-sufficient and give myself the safety and security I needed to speak my truth, no matter the consequences, and feel ok with that in all circumstances.

**My Reflection:** *I want a healthy, intimate relationship, but I need to be in a place within myself where if it doesn't happen, then that is ok too. I can have a life filled with love that does not require a partner, and in this, there is freedom.*

## Your Journey:

1. What needs do you have that you are looking for your partner to fulfill?

2. Where do your needs stem from?

3. How are your needs and the needs of your partner impacting your relationship?

4. What are the unspoken expectations in your relationship?

5. What needs can you fulfill for yourself?

6. How are you modifying your behavior to accommodate your partner's needs in a healthy or unhealthy way?

7. Describe how your personal needs help or hinder your relationship.

8. What are the needs of your relationship?

9. In what ways can you take responsibility for your own happiness?

## Your Reflection:

Having allowed some time to pass since working with the prompts and re-reading your responses, ask yourself:

What stands out for me is .......................................................

The recurring patterns I can see are ........................................

My learning is .......................................................................

My next step will be .............................................................

# GRIEVING THE LOSS

*"It's ok to get angry."*

## My Journey:

There is much to unpack in the ending of a relationship. Firstly, I had to grieve the loss. I was losing a man that I loved, and I was losing our future together. I was losing the intact family unit. I was losing a home, a community, a known reality, and I was losing my determination that our relationship would last.

Our relationship had been on life-support for many years when we finally decided to pull the plug. I knew it could no longer be resuscitated. The final ending of our relationship felt like a death. How can two people who love each other not be together? Why couldn't it be that simple? But, it wasn't.

I was angry at the way my husband had treated me, angry that I had allowed him to, and angry at the fact that I was now going to need to live alone when it was the last thing I wanted to do. I was angry that we had become just another statistic of failed marriages, and I was angry that I was powerless to fix any of it.

I was angry that I would have to go to all of the familiar places alone. Even going to the grocery store felt heavy and a reminder of the "couple" things we would do together. I remember the feeling of walking into our home after my husband had left with all of his belongings. I stepped into the sheer horror of an empty shell inside me and surrounding me. An energy was missing, a heartbeat beside me, a hand to hold, lips to kiss, the sound of conversation in the air. All that remained was a huge silent void, amidst a darkness weighted with sadness, fear, and loneliness, and with no known future in sight.

I felt like years and years of my life had been wasted trying to be what everyone else needed me to be. I had compromised myself to the point of unrecognition. Who was I without my husband? Who was I without my children at home? Who was I without my home? I had become invisible in my own life and I was in disbelief at how I had allowed this to happen.

I was filled with anger and resentment, an energy that had been brooding inside of me for many years. Each time we broke up, sold our home, and bought a new one, we took a financial hit, depleting us to the point where there was not much equity left when dividing our assets for the final time.

My husband had a good, steady job, so his ability to bounce back financially would be much easier than mine. It is a sad reality for many women when a marriage ends, that their financial status drops, sometimes to the point of poverty. Faced with a decline in household income, and an unfulfilling job that was making me sick, I would come to the decision later that I would need to sell my home, a journey I share in *"Journal Through the Journey of Letting Go of Your Home."*

I gave myself space to feel my anger and to express it. I screamed in my car, into my pillow and raged into my journal, anything I could do to get it out. I knew that if I allowed it, it could become all consuming and the anger and resentment would ultimately hurt me and my ability to move forward. I wanted to become better, not bitter. I had to get it out, get all of it out, and then go forward.

The decision to end the marriage would set me on a solitary journey that, although I initially resented it, would be a pivotal turning point in my life.

I forgave my husband, because although I was the recipient of his woundedness, I understood his behavior, reactions, and actions. I understood the impact of his past on his present. I understood the internal programming and challenges one must overcome to live in some form of "normal."

I was not raging at him, I was raging at the outcome of a traumatic childhood that ravaged his heart and psyche, and that would deem him, without doing his own internal healing, incapable of receiving the love he deserved.

I chose not to focus on his behavior, but rather on what was underneath the surface and driving his behavior and mine as well. We were both good people, and we were both wounded people trying to the best of our ability to navigate a marriage.

**My Reflection:** *Anger can be a motivator for change. It sends us signals that something needs to be addressed and action needs to be taken. But when ignored or unexpressed, it will infuse itself into perceptions and behaviors and undermine relationships. I needed to acknowledge my anger, take appropriate action, and then I needed to let it go.*

## Your Journey:

1. Name what you are needing to let go of.

2. What losses are you experiencing by letting go?

3. What anger and resentment are you hanging onto?

4. What has your anger been trying to tell you?

5. Give a voice to your grief.

6. How will letting go impact your life?

7. How can you view your partner with a more compassionate lens?

8. What does letting go of anger and resentment feel like in your body?

9. Describe what forgiveness looks like for you.

## Your Reflection:

Having allowed some time to pass since working with the prompts and re-reading your responses, ask yourself:

What stands out for me is ....................................................

The recurring patterns I can see are ........................................

My learning is ..............................................................

My next step will be ........................................................

# ENDING YOUR RELATIONSHIP WELL

*"Infuse integrity into all that you do."*

## My Journey:

What did it take to end a relationship well? It took a lot of integrity and a lot of letting go. It was about acknowledging and honoring my experience of the relationship as well as my husband's. Had my husband shared his journey with you, it would have been a different version of the same story.

I believe the energy we bring to endings translates into the energy of our new beginnings. To turn love into hate and resentment causes more harm and suffering to people who have already suffered enough.

The years with my husband were not all bad and need not be tainted with a bitter focused recollection. There were many good times, tender times, thoughtful times, fun times, that I continue to choose as the narrative through which to see him, and our now friendship.

There were very real, very valid reasons why the relationship did not work for both of us. In sharing the ending of my relationship with you, my intent was not to paint a picture of my husband as the persecutor and I the victim, but rather to give insight to what is happening underneath the surface of reactions and behaviors, and to show how, if left unhealed, or at the very least unexamined, our past greatly impacts our present and our ability to have success in our relationships.

We successfully navigated parting ways, with our respect for each other intact. We spend time together with family on many occasions and events throughout the year and feel the benefits for everyone, including ourselves. In being inclusive rather than separate, we have reinvented a workable family relationship for us all, one we are both very proud of.

At the time of this writing, it has been seven years since my marriage ended. Seven years of being on my own, getting reacquainted with myself, doing my healing inner work, selling my home, quitting my job and traveling across Canada, going on safari in South Africa, living in an ashram in India, venturing to Italy, and working in the far north of Baffin Island. All of this gave me the time, focus, and clarity within myself to become a successful life coach and published author.

I would not have been able to accomplish what I have, had I stayed in the toxic cycle of my marriage. I needed to be on my own and know that I could make it on my own. This built in me, a belief and trust in myself and my abilities that I did not have before. In letting go of everything, I found myself. I opened myself up to so many new and wonderful possibilities, things I would never have experienced had I stayed.

The ending of a relationship is terrifyingly hard, but if done with love and integrity, each person can choose to emerge with the dignity and clarity to move forward into their own new chapter. There was enough wounding in our relationship, the ending did not need to wound us as well.

**My Reflection:** *I learned many things from my husband, things that helped me to become a better person, and he learned from me as well. We may not have made it as a couple, in the traditional sense, but we mastered ending it well, thus allowing us a solid friendship as we moved forward alone.*

### Your Journey:

1.  What does ending your relationship well look like for you?

2.  What do you need to let go of in order to end your relationship well?

3.  Describe what you have learned about yourself in your relationship.

4.  Write out a summary of your relationship as you experienced it.

5.  Write out a summary of your partner's experience in the relationship.

6. What are some of the things you are thankful for?

7. How can you be supported in ending your relationship well?

8. Where do you need to create healthy boundaries in letting go?

9. What vision do you have for your new chapter?

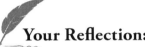

## Your Reflection:

Having allowed some time to pass since working with the prompts and re-reading your responses, ask yourself:

What stands out for me is ........................................................

The recurring patterns I can see are ........................................

My learning is ........................................................................

My next step will be ..............................................................

# FINAL
# THOUGHTS

## My Final Thoughts:

Ending my 20-year relationship was an excruciatingly long and difficult journey, but it was necessary. Could I have left once, never to return, absolutely not. Not much in life is cut and dry, or black and white. When things are hard we usually need to follow a process of decline to the point of no return.

The relationship unraveled and collapsed in stages as the foundation upon which it was built began to disintegrate. I tried desperately to hang on, to patch up the holes, to wish and hope my way into its restoration, but the truth was, we were on a trajectory towards its demise, and we did not have the tools to fix it.

I finally had to surrender to the fact that my relationship was filled with too much history and heartache to be resurrected and that what I needed most was a fresh start.

## Your Final Thoughts:

Now it's your turn to reflect upon your journey through working with this book. Take some time to write out your concluding thoughts. This will be a summary of your learning, insights,

and aha moments. This is your opportunity to capture and record whatever has resonated with you. This can be a valuable and personal resource for you to use in the years ahead as you face the new journeys your life will offer.

Here are some prompts to help guide you:

1. What are the key takeaways that you have uncovered within yourself on this journey?

2. How has going on this Journaling Journey changed your perception of yourself and your relationships?

3. How has this journey changed your outlook?

4. How has writing your way through this journey impacted your ability to see yourself?

5. Envision the life that you desire. What will it take to get from where you are to where you want to be?

6. What patterns and programming will you need to let go of?

7. Describe what you will need to support you in embarking on your journey of transformation.

…Continued

8.  How has this Journaling Journey helped to give you clarity?

9.  What will your next journey be?

# CONCLUSION

I hope that through this journey you have come to know yourself better, and have felt supported through reading my journey and working through the writing prompts, and have the strength and determination to take those necessary steps to move yourself forward and create the life that you both deserve and desire.

As a regular practice, journaling is a great way to stay connected to your truth, to have a record of your experiences, to work through challenges to triumph, and to see the progress that you are making within yourself and your life.

For additional support in your life transitions, I invite you to try more *Journaling Journeys*, as an integral part of your health and well-being.

If you feel that you need further support, I would be happy to speak with you about your journey and how my coaching services may be of benefit to you. I can be reached at Linda@inwardboundcoaching.com.

I would also love your feedback and invite you to leave an honest review of this book at www.amazon.com.

This will help me with future offerings as well as support other women on their journey through change, self-discovery and personal growth.

# ACKNOWLEDGEMENTS

It takes a village to raise an author. I must firstly thank my friend and editor, Judy, who has walked my entire journey with me and whose friendship, encouragement, and belief in me has carried me through many years. Without her wisdom, guidance, and support, this series of books would not exist.

I also would like to thank Bob, my ex-husband, who continues to be a support and a man who exemplifies loving-kindness, loyalty, honesty, and living with integrity.

Thank you to my children, Ian, Heather and Caitlin, they are my heart outside of my body who inspire me to be the best I can be, and for my granddaughter Brooklynn who is a bright light, and brings us all such joy and nuggets of wisdom.

Thank you to my beloved mother, Joyce, who is now *somewhere over the rainbow* and watches over me, cheering me on.

Thank you to Shayne, Timm and the "Golden Girls" for the love and laughter that has carried me through.

Thank you to Alx, Michael, Kim, and Sandra, who have infused their beauty and wisdom into my life.

And finally, I have to thank the members of my publishing tribe: Jacob, Ed, Zsoka, Fiona, Sue, Wendy, Christiana, Richard, Zoe, and Eithne, who have inspired and encouraged me through my publishing journey.

# ADDITIONAL JOURNALING JOURNEYS

**Journal Through the Journey of...**

Letting Go of Your Home
Changing Your Career
Accepting Your Child's Journey
Moving Toward Your Health and Wellness

For new additions to the *Journaling Journeys* Series, check out:

www.journalingjourneys.com
www.inwardboundcoaching.com

For more information on journeys and coaching, please email:

Linda@inwardboundcoaching.com

The journey continues…

Made in the USA
Monee, IL
24 November 2022

17871684R00076